I0436543

We Rise

Printed by CreateSpace

Published by Odaine Tomlinson at Smashwords

Copyright 2014 Odaine Tomlinson

Smashwords Edition, License Notes

"We should say to the millions who are in Afri[k]a to hold the fort, for we are coming 400 million strong." ~ Marcus Garvey

Contents

Note to reader: The bolded & underlined information within these chapters are YouTube videos you can look up to view

<u>Open To Your Words</u>

I give the knowledge and wisdom to you the reader, which has been passed down to me amongst those who have gone before me and my great ancestors of Afrika. Feel free to do your own research and due diligence on any topic addressed in this eBook. As I have learned from the teachings of Dr Ray Hagins; NO EVIDENCE NO ARGUMENT.

*Special thanks to @heyyoungworld01 for correcting my mistake on this eBook cover from 'Ferguson, MI 2014' to 'St. Louis, MO 2014' based on evidence of geographic location and misrepresentation.

Integration: The Demise of Our People

<u>What no one wants to say about Ferguson</u>! – Length: 03:42 –
Contains Mild Explicit Content

Michael Brown, Treyvon Martin, Fred Hampton, Malcolm X, Medgar Evans, and Harry More, are all black people throughout history who have used their blood to unify the people. There is a reason that I choose not to acknowledge Memphis, TN 1968. This represents the assassination of Martin Luther King Junior. Contrary to popular belief Martin Luther King was not a proper influence to the uprising of the Afrikans in America. He was and will always be remembered as the leader (a passive leader) who asked for permission to change from those who caused the same reason for the need of change. This is why he is falsely recognized as a hero in the black community.

Don't believe me? Well take a look at Google. If you Google every person I just mentioned above, you will clearly see an assassination date clearly stated. While when you Google Martin Luther King Junior, you see him represented as a shrine underneath the date of his holiday. Of all the people I have mentioned above; Martin Luther King is the only one who has a federal recognized holiday.

As you can see through history by now, marching and protesting is insufficient to any cause. With any cause; by marching and protesting you are asking permission to carry out your cause. If you were to march and protest your employment position, you would be asking permission from the ones who ignored your request to reconsider. This in turn; by being so submissive, gives them the power to ignore you over and over again. Perhaps that's why in the heart of every 'rough' state, there is a Martin Luther King Jr. Blvd as a reminder to idea of asking permission.

This is why Martin Luther King can never be acknowledged as a leader who stood up for the overall progression of black people. Integrating for the sake of compromising rights is not the answer in any situation. Therefore, the steps of black nation building inside this eBook serve as the first of many steps to realistic equal rights and justice for black people around the world. Once our eyes are all open as a whole; then and only then; WE RISE!

Melanin Strong

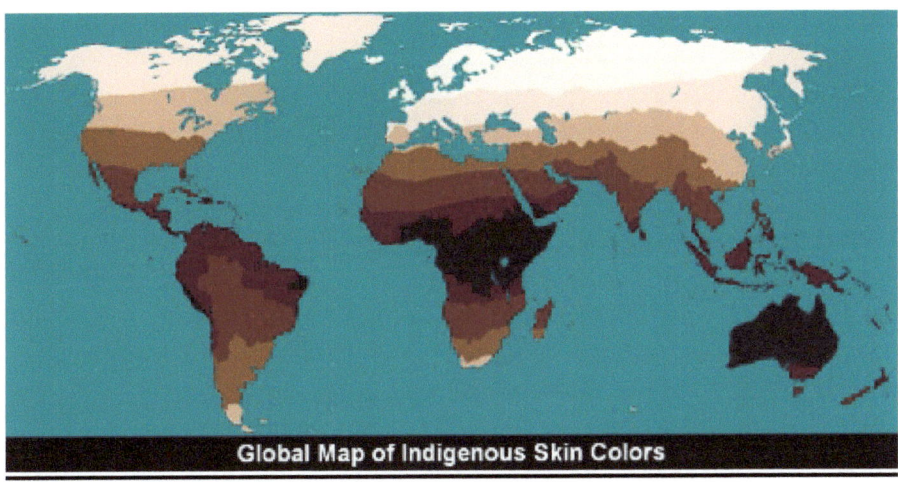

Global Map of Indigenous Skin Colors

We; the Afrikans of the world are the most valuable forms of existence to this planet. We have the highest level of melanin; which gives us higher levels of thought, awareness, and movement than any other race on the planet. The darker your skin the more melanin you have; while those who are the most melanin deficient, who are known as Caucasians or white people, have insignificant levels of melanin compared to black Afrikans. Melanin, or the deficiency of it, is the pigment or hormone that gives every human being on the planet their skin color; hair color; and eye color. Believe it or not; the most natural form of human beings from the beginning of the creation of earth were people of melanin rich bodies; BLACK PEOPLE. Black people have ruled the earth for thousands and thousands of years. It wasn't until our melanin rich, black ancestors of the human race began traveling and migrating to other lands outside of Afrika, that the creation, spread, and destruction of human beings of melanin deficiency multiplied into existence. This means that people of ALL ethnic races are derived from the original state of human beings, which have always been black people.

Also, those who are 'melanin strong' have higher levels of spirituality connectivity; along with higher connectivity with electromagnetic frequencies in and around them. Also, those who are 'melanin strong', can naturally absorb the effects of the sun rays on their skin; while those who are melanin deficient must often times use sun block to avoid harmful effects from the sun, due to the inability of their melanin content to properly use the sun's nutrients.

Melanin is produced in the center of every human being's brain; no matter the color of their skin. This location of production is called the pineal gland, also known as the third eye in a spiritual reference. Yet truth be told, some religions try to ignore the existence of the pineal gland by associating it with 'the devil'. Therefore, I wish to expose the secrets to why and how this is done in the depths of this factual based eBook. But for now, I would like for you to understand that you are the result of the melanin that flows through your body. Black people hold dominance over any other race on every level, yet black people are the only race who do not know the secrets of their own history and are unaware of today's systematic exploitation, that I also reveal in these writings. Now that you are more aware of the power of the melanin that runs through your veins; take the rest of this journey through this eBook with your third eye open.

Imagine That

PRE-SLAVERY
-Afrika
-Peace
-Prosperity
-Power
-Kemetic Spirituality
-UNITY

SLAVERY
-Destruction
-No Peace
-Rape/Torture
-Massacres
-New Language & Ideal Religion

POST-SLAVERY
-Inferiority
-Segragation
-NonRecognition as Citizens Under Declaration of Independance
-UnEqual Justice
-NO UNITY

FOLLOWED BY
-Post Traumatic Slave Syndrome
-No Knowledge Of Ancestors
-Claim English & Christianity As Our Own Culture
-NO UNTIY

Imagine that you are at home playing your favorite videogame, doing your favorite hobby, or just relaxing with your family. All of a sudden; someone kicks down your door and terrorizes your home with excessive force and vandalism. Then you and your family are tied up and kidnapped against your will for human trafficking; possibly never seeing your family ever again. Imagine that happening to you right now. How would you handle it? What would you do? And could you even do anything?

Now imagine reaching an unknown destination where the people who kidnapped you speak, read, and write a different language from you. Imagine the feeling of hopelessness and confusion as random people spit on you; rape you at will; torment your remaining loved ones; and also redefine all things that you have grown accustomed to in your life. It can be a very scary image. But take it even further; let's imagine that centuries go by, but your people are still innocently killed, neglected and worked until their painful death. Now imagine that half of the people of this foreign land continue to violate you and reap the benefits of your forced labor, while the other half of the people upgrade your level of significance from a worthless slave to an undermined labor expense. Your enslaved people as a whole later become free; at least that's what you're told; but you realize that you were never freed on principles of humanity respects. You were freed because half of the people who had to pay for your labor were upset with those who had your unlimited labor for free; causing the creation of the Emancipation Proclamation to equalize the playing field of those who had to pay nothing for your forced way of life.

Also, as a matter of fact; the very people, who created this chaos and destruction of the original people of the world, are the very same group of people who have the least amount of melanin in their body. Those who are melanin deficient tend to exert more unnatural destruction and chaos. Throughout history, those who are of the least melanin count have created the most destruction to planet earth and themselves; which the Roman Coliseum shows great truth to this amongst many others.

Can you imagine the despair that the people who suffer from this type of torment have to carry? We; the black people have suffered tremendously in the recent centuries. Yet, we; the black people must recognize the glitch that has been placed in the time of the human race; so therefore we of all races can once again live and let live. Imagine the thousands of years of history that black people have ruled and the peace that was in the world during this previous time. This is the type of information that you will not learn or hear about in traditional education. Can you imagine why? Do you think the people who are pulling these strings are melanin strong or melanin deficient?

The Culture of Hip-Hop

Hip Hop was created and carried on by those who were melanin strong; BLACK PEOPLE. The very foundation of Hip-Hop is conscious lyricism, meaning; the ability to express a conscious story in the form of music. At its best, melanin plays a huge role in the creation and creativity used to freestyle and make strong lyrical content that others gain wisdom from. Also; just as important; Hip Hop is a way for black people to use our skills to communicate to and through our community. Hip Hop has always spoken to and for the culture; which is the essence of what Hip-Hop is.

Sadly, there are people today who claim to be a part of the culture who provide no respect to the culture; this included people who are black and white. One of the greatest conscious Hip Hop lyricists dead or alive is Canibus. There is no human being on earth in the Hip Hop culture who can compare to his lyricism; Canibus - Poet Laureate Infinity 1000 bars serves as ultimate proof to this.

However, there is an issue; the people who have owned the major record labels of today ARE NOT black. This means that they do not collectively have the inbred will or desire to respect the black culture of Hip Hop. Because of this, Hip Hop has been watered down since the early 90's to eliminate the use of melanin rich lyrical content. Furthermore, what this means is that since the culture has been broken down and redefined; anyone TODAY who does not provide strong lyrical content can step onto the scene and claim a spot in today's broken down version of Hip Hop. Here is a prime example of what Hip Hop is now being systematically turned into; **Iggy Azalea - Work (Explicit)** Length 03:48 Strong Explicit Content

I personally have much love for true Hip Hop. I have seen Hip Hop at its best and Hip Hop at its worst. Yet, the very artists who have the power to bring Hip Hop back to the way it was intended to be are silent, some are even endorsing this systematic change. And to be 100% honest, Hip Hop is literally turning into Pop music. Once again, the originality that black people have created, has been stripped away and redefined. But in all reality, we as black people have to take part of the blame. Why aren't we as a black people using our money, lyricism and power to create our own record labels to make music for the best interest of our people and our culture; instead of the best interest of greed performed by the melanin deficient today?

For all the rappers and producers who sold out Hip Hop, and the fans who need a wakeup call; I dedicate this video to you: **Hopsin - ILL MIND OF HOPSIN 5** Length: 05:06 Strong Explicit Content

Gang Banging 101

For all the black men and women of the world who gangbang, there seems to be common reasons for why they bang; Respect, protection, neighborhood security and guidance, are some of the main reasons. And truthfully, some gangbang to have pride in their flag to call their own, while others are forced into it from peer pressure. But whether you're a part of the original or related versions of Bloods or Crips; I have three simple questions you need to ask yourself. Who is the most respected gang banger of all time? Which gang came first and why; bloods or crips? What is the foundation of the bloods and crips?

Sadly, a lot of black people who claim to live or die by their gang have no idea of the history of what they represent past their neighborhoods most original OG. Well I hope that after these words, if you happen to be a gangbanger or know someone who is; that there can now be a greater understanding for needed change.

The most respected gang banger of all time is Stanley Tookie Williams III; the co-founder of the Crips gang and highest ranked OG of all OG's up until December 13, 2005. Tookie was highly feared and respected along with the founder of the Crip gang Raymond Washington. Not too long after battling along with the notorious formation of the Bloods for the streets of Los Angeles; Tookie was imprisoned for multiple crimes. But before I talk about Tookie I have to talk about the source of why black people got involved with gangbanging.

The ultimate source of gangbanging is survival; more specifically survival from oppression. After centuries of inhuman slavery of black people, white supremacy against black people has 'changed forms'. In LA and all over America, black people were 'given some rights' but still targeted with hatred from white people. This hatred and mistreatment caused the formation of The Black Panthers as a form of protection for black communities against racial injustices. However, at the peak of effectiveness, leaders of the Black Panthers were killed systematically. This caused black men of America to have lack of leadership to properly organize for the sake of their cause of protection; which later brought Raymond Washington into the picture who started his own formation that was later called Crips. Back then, your fist gave you credit, so Raymond fought and recruited others to join forces with him. He later linked up with Tookie to expand his gang of Crips against common rivals of other neighborhoods, which formed themselves into Bloods. The Bloods existed because the Crips existed; the Crips existed because of the gap of leadership in the Black Panthers existed; and the Black Panthers existed because of the inhuman actions of torture from white people during and after 'lawful slavery' existed.

Tookie was such an impact to gangbanging and to the world; not only because of his status as the co-founder of the Crips; but because while in prison on death row, he woke up and changed his ways. He realized that his involvement with the creation of the Crips caused an ongoing slaughter of not just innocent people, but black people who were systematically killing themselves blindly instead of living life to the fullest. He later published many books for gang prevention that led to his nomination for the Noble Peace Prize. If you don't know much about Stanley Tookie Williams III, I highly recommend looking into his legacy and the movie dedicated to him called **Redemption - The Stan Tookie Williams Story**. Length 01:33:03 Strong Explicit Content

Here is an excerpt from the movie Redemption dedicated to all gangbangers:

"I had a bad rep; I believed the people, (because they were afraid of me) they respected me. That was a mistake. Respect cannot be earned by using violence to scare people. Many gang bangers are scared all the time but they won't tell anyone because they don't want their homeboys to think that they're not down. Gangbangers live by bad rules; their rules make it OK to be dishonest; their rules make it OK to use violence against others; their rules make it OK to put their own lives in danger; but you; you don't have to live by their rules; you can choose to live by new rules."

For the gangbangers out there, I only ask that you ask yourself this:

If the enemy you're fighting and killing has the same reasons for fighting and killing you, then don't you think it's time for you and your enemy to have the same reasons for working together to get rid of the reasons for fighting and killing?

What Are They Hiding?

Our history runs deep my brothers and sisters, and is also being erased daily. Our Afrikan ancestors have always been the leaders of today's modern civilization. We have many ancestors that significantly outsmarted the so called most intelligent man Albert Einstein. One of our great ancestors Imhotep is the world's first multi-genius. Imhotep is the one and only master of medicine and healing; he is the world's first doctor; the first man of science in recorded history; the first to practice surgery; and the first to master chemistry (which is actually the study of melanin). And if you are wondering; his name should sound familiar to you in this modern world; his name has been horrifically slandered in the movie The Mummy as an evil mummy who returns from the dead who terrorizes the earth. Worst of all in this same movie he is shown as a light skin Arab. IMHOTEP WAS A BLACK MAN FULL OF MELANIN. Why was his character slandered? And why are there so many other examples of our ancestors being slandered on a regular basis, yet we don't stand up to stop it?

If you can find the true answers to these questions below for yourself then you will find the mindboggling truth. Why was Lake Nasser created in Egypt when there were so much more negative than positive results anticipated from it? Was it a coincidence that many hieroglyphics and temples made by our ancestors were covered up by this manmade lake? Why do the faces behind this operation look nothing like the almost 100,000 Nubians who were washed away by this man made dam? Did the faces who built this man-made potential genocide seek the permission and wisdom of the Nubians prior to building; or was there a more lucrative motive?

Why is it that Arabs are performing a silent takeover of Egypt? Why is it that Arabs are being employed by foreign United States and European nations to daily deface and vandalize the temples and writings on the walls left by our ancestors? Why is there significant evidence of our ancestors sacred writings being covered and written over with Christian symbols; but black people of the world are not informed? Well you may want to look up the meaning of Social Darwinism to help find the answers.

Well my brothers and sisters; there is a systematic plot going on right now to destroy the remains of our history to further exploit the abundance of Afrika. Many of the leaders in Afrika know this and do what they can, but without the collective support of black people around the world it turns into a losing battle day by day. Don't take my word for it, look up the facts yourself. Look at powerful actions of Zimbabwe President Mugabe who is kicking out ALL remaining white farmers from his country. Our brothers and sisters near and far, are taking action but we still have much work to do. The time for our mental awakening is now. The current monetary system for you to tap into at this very moment that puts a value of at least ten times greater on your money compared to foreign lands outside of Afrika. I will later explain the logic of this system, to shift the power of black people from world minorities to world authorities (economically). For the longest, we as black people have been the unrecognized innovators of the world. It's time for us to harness our energies and skills under one cause on our own grounds. You have much more power than you think, my brothers and sisters.

The Man Worth $400,000,000,000

The richest man you never knew; Mansa Musa. A great black man who holds the title of unsurpassed wealth ranked at four hundred billion dollars. And did I mention that he was a black man? Mansa Musa was the Emperor of the Mali Empire, and was known for his generosity of giving away thousands on top of thousands of gold bars to other countries on his way to Mecca in Afrika. His legacy, leadership, and generosity were outstanding; but don't you find it strange that the richest man to ever be known in human existence is hardly, if at all, mentioned in public schools? Don't you find it strange that if you search for information about him on the internet that you find very little information about him? Well I find that very strange; but I know that our unity of black people on a global force will once again develop the wealth and prosperity of the black race.

How can I be so sure? Well if you take a look at the median of exchange called fiat money, or paper money; the truth is, it's all fake. The paper money that countries use today has absolutely no tangible value, it is only worth something because our governments passed a law saying that it is. But with Afrika there is a difference; yes there is fiat currency in Afrika as well; but Afrika has the source of the world's natural resources. Afrika has the finest values of the Earth but is blindly depicted as some type of wasteland in the eyes of some. This does not mean Afrika needs to be exploited, just simply cherished and acknowledged for its nature and history.

Well how do we bring the culture, prosperity, and peace back to Afrika? Well my answer is precise and simple. Stop supporting others who have no interest in our well being and start supporting ourselves; buy black; support your brothers and sisters who are up and coming who provide a product or service that you currently use. Once we tap into the 1.1 trillion dollar buying power that we as black people provide to others who are not black; you will see just how important the voice of black people will become to the rest of the world. You will see just how valuable you are to the world and to your brother and sisters.

But while doing this; you can support Afrika while multiplying the value of your dollars by ten times its worth. How? With something called fractional reserve. With fractional reserve, banks have the power to lend out ten times the amount of each dollar you put into a bank account. So that money that you may currently have in Bank of America, Wells Fargo, etc, are owned by people who are not black, is using ten times the amount of your money towards further manipulation and destruction of the world at large.

Now imagine if instead of putting your money into these banks that have no interest in your wellbeing; you open up a bank account online that's based and owned by Afrika and Afrikan people; for example the *Black Star Line Cooperative Credit Union*. Meaning that you still have access to your money, but now the benefit of fractional reserve is in favor of black people. Now also imagine that we and others become wiser financially as people and use this fractional reserve power to our benefit to build onto the progression of Afrika through innovation.

There is nothing stopping us from accomplishment greatness right where we currently live as well as in Afrika; nothing except the unity of our minds to all see the same picture of growth, unity, and peace once again. As a result of the aftermath of foreigners destroying and dividing the unity of Afrika and black people abroad; the unity that once was in Afrika now needs improvement. We; the black people of the world, are the only ones who will stand up for the good of our people; no one else.

Equal Humanity or Black Unity

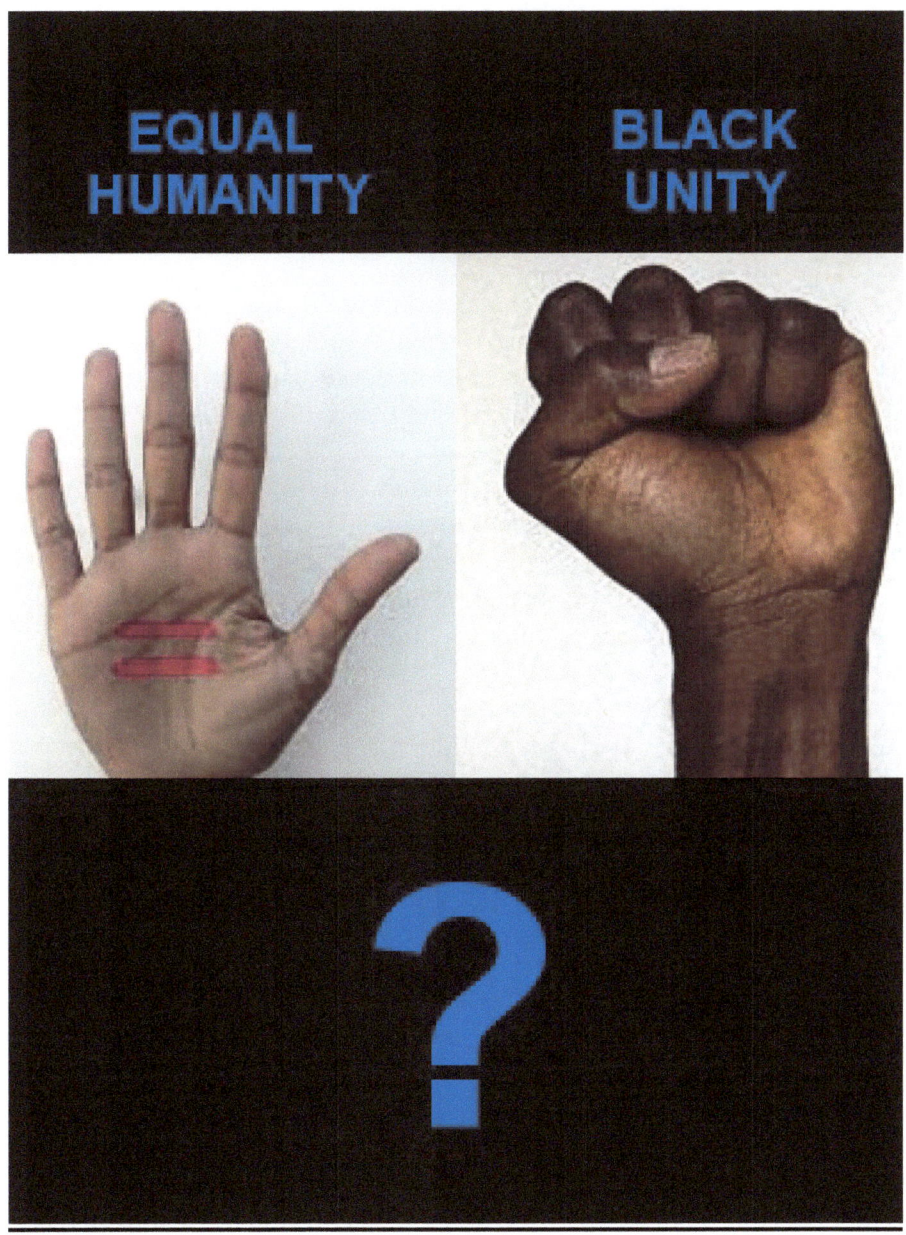

Being Pro-Black does not mean Anti-White. Being Pro-Black simply means that you have the knowledge and self dignity to respect the lifestyle of the black culture. Anti-Black means disregarding the knowledge and lifestyle of black people. Pro-White means having the knowledge and self dignity to respect the lifestyle of the white culture. While Anti-White means disregarding the knowledge and lifestyle of white culture.

Take it upon yourself to analyze those four meanings and ask yourself which meaning is being carried out by your community and by your government. In most cases, Anti-Black & Pro-White is being taught to you by society. Yet, society wants black people to disregard their own identity to support equal rights. The only way black people can support equal rights in a society is when that same society promotes Pro-Blackness just as equally as it promotes their own Pro-Race in that respective society. Therefore, if you are confused about whether or not equality should be the focus over black unity; simply ask yourself if the identity of black culture is being taught to you by the society that wants an equal fight for equal human rights. And to go deeper into this; equal humanity can only exist when all cultures are respected and taught in all schools throughout the world. Stop fooling yourself and other human beings to thinking otherwise.

Why is it that out of every race on the planet, the original human race of black people has no idea who they are? Well modern day slavery plays a huge part in that. But it's up to us to be Pro-Black from now on. As we can all see from the world's example; no one else is going to teach black people to be proud of black people EXCEPT for black people.

This does not mean to stoop to the level of playing tit for tat with other races. Just focus on the growth of your people while respecting the other cultures around the planet. What I have sadly seen is that black people who have been traumatized by the people who are severely Anti-Black; have hid wrongly hid behind the idea of being Pro-Black. They believe that they are Pro-Black for demonizing white people; but in some cases they actually spend their life being Anti-White; where they focus on their outward hate. But they also spend so much time being Anti-White with their life that they never take the time to actually be Pro-Black by learning about their own history and adding to the progression of their people instead of spreading hate. It needs to also be stated that learning and informing other people of our history is not spreading hate; it is educating ourselves and remembering what we came from; so we can assess where we are going.

So I encourage you to keep these definitions in mind. An equal humanity may one day come, but between now and then, we have plenty of work to do on our own as black people. Let others do their things while we unite to regain our own identity. I once heard from Bobby Hemmitt that 'even a roach knows that it's a roach'; yet we as black people are just waking up to who we are in this information age.

Modern Day Slavery

Are we still in slavery today? Well some may argue that since black people are no longer being slashed with whips, that all is forgotten. Some even say that black people are wrong for constantly bringing up the past; but the same people that oppose bringing this up are the same people who have no personal experience of the generational effects it had on our recent ancestors; and in most cases those same people may have family members who were distributing these barbaric actions.

But just to be absolutely clear, modern day slavery is in full effect this very day. You can tell by the few black people who have a sense of feeling inferior to 'the white man' yet they don't know that it is actually 'the white man' who is inferior to us. There is a sense amongst some slavery minded black people, of backing down from the false image of 'the white man'. Yet, I guarantee that if these very same slavery minded black people spent the time to read this eBook, let alone hop on YouTube, Google, or their favorite Social Network in search of the history of black people, they will learn that there is nothing about black people that makes us any lesser than the so called 'white man'. This is not the 15th to 19th century. Our ancestors have felt the pain of being and feeling inferior; so we must not carry that burden anymore; it's time to move forward. We are in the 21st century; meaning that there should be no reason why black people should be blind to the truth.

Another example of modern day slavery is today's prison system; primarily America and Europe. Our black men have been heavily targeted since the destruction of Hip Hop, introduction of cocaine, and other negative 'introductions' before and during the early 1990's. There is a mind boggling increase in the number of people imprisoned in America and Europe; especially in America; and especially black people. The prison system has tremendously evolved and is turning into a concentration camp for black people specifically. Don't believe me? Well take a look at this short and mind boggling video **US Prison System By the Numbers** Length 03:40

Also, there is the systematic manipulation of European and Eurocentric standards that is pressured onto our black people around the world. I once heard it said that, the worst example of slavery is a Black Man with a European mind. Some black people have no idea that their minds are Europeanized today. The greatest form of this is a self hating black man or black woman that finds no beauty in one's own culture; a black man who is feminized; or a black man who dresses like a woman. We need to flush all this nonsense and unify to exchange our origins to grow our people.

One of the biggest forms of modern day slavery is our unjust inability in some countries of self expression of our black culture. Why is it that it is frowned upon in corporate America to have facial hair or a certain amount of natural hair length for black men or black woman? Why is it that wearing a hijab is acknowledged by corporate America, yet black people must abide by the standards of white America. Why is it that we have no say in our right to be our natural selves? Well if you didn't know, there is somewhere you can be as black as you would like to be to embrace your black culture. And that is in Afrika, the motherland. Also as a heads up, America and Europe has been playing a huge role in lying to black people by giving us the idea that Afrika is a wasteland that is full of people who have no clue to the rest of the world. Well my brothers and sisters; in The Rebirth of Afrikan Innovation chapter you will see two short videos dated in 2008 & 2014 that proves to the truth of the thriving Afrikan culture and high lead in technological advancement. Let the truth be told that Afrika is ready for the unity of black people around the world; and let it be told that we must begin to humble ourselves and flush the junk that has been brainwashed to us as a black people in order to embrace our welcome.

From Women of Royalty to Peasants

I humbly say that I feel ashamed to the fact that the beautiful Afrikan woman of today outside of Afrika; primarily in America, has been horrifically exploited and visually vandalized by the European idea of beauty along with the need to exploit ourselves to gain a false sense of power and success. Nothing is more beautiful than the divine essence that the black woman brings to this world and also to the progress of mankind and the universe. For thousands of years Afrikan women have enjoyed more rights, freedom, and liberty more than any other race throughout any period of time; including today. Afrikan women had the respected power and authority that most Europeans cannot fathom even today.

As my lovely wife and Goddess has told me, "If a woman becomes lost, then her nation is not too far behind." It is no wonder that black people have had no sense of unity for the longest. And the reason for this is the uninvited systematic insertion of European ideals into the minds of black women. For the women of the world who falsely idolize today's black woman; who have sold their dignity and soul to money and fame; and to the woman who are currently doing it; take a look at this: **Who Is Sara Baartman? Every black woman should know her name** Length 04:56

Shocking to say the least; what's even more shocking is that this European idea of disgracing our black woman is alive and thriving today. When I see black women who try their hardest to look white instead of embracing their natural beauty of blackness, it saddens me. The black women of today need to wake up and realize just how important it is for them to be black, be proud, and be beautiful. Never sacrifice your beauty just to be perm-haired, pro-blonde, and pro-plastic surgery. And what's even more horrific is that there are some black men in America who are jumping on the bandwagon to try to look like a white woman as well. I think I have the right to say that this is absolutely ridiculous. Wake up black empresses of the world! You are beautiful!

Don't let the white and lost black people destroy and humiliate the character of the black goddess in you. You are better than that. In fact you are the best, the original woman of this planet; and I support that statement with thousands of years of evidence left around the planet by our ancestors.

You deserve to be treated as the goddess you were created to be. Start now to open your eyes to the black woman within, to relearn the characteristics of the black women of royalty who have gone before you. And don't forget to help your fellow black women along that way. The black men of the world who are already or changing into self proclaimed kings are waiting for your transformation. The black men of the world are counting on you. Once our black women are strong and know their value, then the black men can stand even taller and further unite globally to progress our evolution as one.

The Ultimate Control of Black People

(The picture below is an anonymous reality check)

For black people to believe in the same God that allow them to be enslaved, shows their level of intelligence. We are living in the age of INFORMATION! Why are they still believers? It makes no sense. We gave blacks christianity because it made them better slaves. Even my great grandpa told my dad once that blacks accepting Christianity was the best thing that ever happened to white slavers. The fear of Hell and promise of everlasting life is what finally kept the slaves from rebelling and running away. Lol and now days black people are still praising the very imaginary white guy who allowed them to be enslaved in the first place. Shouting and dancing with their wigs falling off in church lol. I'm no racist but we all must admit that black Christian women are some funny m[***********]s. The only whites who believe in Christianity are the descendants of poor whites from those days. The rich whites didn't believe in that crap because they knew what it was being used for. Control over the slaves and poor whites

♥ 26 likes

Ask yourself this…

Why would you accept the religion of someone who goes out of their way to kill and destroy your way of life in the name of their religion?

Let's start from the beginning. Before there were wars and invasions; there were black people. Black people lived peacefully in Afrika and practiced Kemetic spirituality for thousands and thousands of years. It wasn't until Ptolemy I Soter conquered Egypt, that religion came into existence in Afrika. With this rule, Soter wanted to be worshipped as a god so he invented a sculpture for people of Egypt to worship as god; naming it Serapis in 350 B.C.E; to later be named Serapis Christus. This man made god was later reclaimed and renamed under the rule of Roman Emperor Constantine and the Council of Nicea based on the uprising of the worshipers of Serapis who were called Christians. So Constantine made it law that the image of Serapis be worshiped as Jesus Christ and its worshipers be acknowledged as Christians. Meaning, that Jesus Christ does not exist; he was created for the purpose of Europeanization of the world to follow. Don't get mad at me or take my word for it; look up the information in these previous sentences on your own. This is the absolute foundation of Christianity that has been manipulated and reformed over time to its most effective stage of mentally enslaving black people of the world.

Meanwhile, back in Afrika, about 300 years after Christianity was made law by Constantine; Khalif Omar, who was an advisor to Muhammad; invaded and conquered Egypt with his Islamic troops and created a widespread of the new religion of Islam into Afrikan culture. During Khalif's reign in power, the religion of Islam became very widespread in North Afrika; which was the birth of today's current Arab nation silent and growing presence in Northern Afrika.

Even today, black people have accepted and respected the religion of those who have terrorized their family members and Afrika. Yet for thousands of years before invasions, Afrikans practiced peaceful spirituality, compared to today's handful recent religions that caused chaos. If our ancestors have laid the mindboggling ground work for civilization, then don't you find it strange that with the recent religions and chaos put onto us and planet earth that something doesn't add up?

I hope you can look into that answer for yourself. But two things I must add is the fact that there is no room for exploitation and capital gain in spirituality; yet there is plenty of that and more with every religion. Also, the shortest and fastest way between two points is a straight line. This means that adding a third point would delay the transfer and leave room for unintended manipulation as well as miscommunication through that third point. I urge you to use your right to think. Your choice of prayer is strictly yours to choose from; I only ask that if you feel a certain way; to look into the absolute foundation of your faith to ensure the solidity of its principles.

It is actually amazing just how great Afrika really is. The first form of human speech, writing, medicine, surgery, architecture, mathematics, mineral mining, iron smelting, philosophy, international trade, and art, all originated from Afrika. In spite of the destruction of Afrika from foreign nations, the foundational beauty of Afrika still remains. Contrary to the subliminal messages that America and Europe have portrayed, Afrikan entrepreneurship is on the rise. The leaders of Afrika are working more effectively to see that Afrika becomes the great nation of peace and prosperity for the future generations to come. Here is a look at Afrika's level of innovation in year 2014: **Africa 2014 | Forging Inclusive Growth, Creating Jobs** Length 03:13

As you can see, Afrika is moving forward tremendously. We still have our internal areas of needs for improvement that we as a people must address; but I know that once we as black people can all unify and come together on a global scale that our country can one day live in total prosperity and peace once again. And to help propel this, Afrikan governments are currently evicting people out of Afrikan countries who have been exploiting the land and progress of Afrika for their own greedy gains. This means that Afrikan ethics is being pushed to the forefront once again to ensure the forward movement of Afrikan people as a whole. This also means that not every black person outside of Afrika will be welcomed into Afrika. Believe it or not, some black people are so Europeanized that they will not want to humble themselves to change their way of thinking. I myself agree 100% that the black people who do not want to contribute to Afrika in a positive way, should not consider residing in Afrika. There has been enough chaos and exploitation brought to Afrika, so if you know you would like to be accepted all you have to do is to first find yourself. Find out who you really are, while also flushing out the influence of European ideas that you have been taught. This means changing and improving the way you think, speak, eat, and act to bring out the Afrikan in you. This also means you may have to change your circle of friends. Get around other people that will bring you up mentally, emotionally, and spiritually. We need to focus on black unity; not black separation.

There are many things that black people of the world can contribute to Afrika. Afrika is in very high demand for black business owners around the world to come to Afrika to contribute to growth; so long as they know themselves first. A continent full of active melanin is destined to thrive in all areas of life; it is the law of nature. Black people helping black communities across Afrika; black people giving their extra to other black people to build their progress, to eventually do the same to someone else; this is the foundation of our success. We stand tall and united; we create a conglomerate of our own black Afrikan made products and services to share with Afrika and the world, for the benefit of Afrikan people, by Afrikan people.

I myself have thought of many ideas. One of which is, where as more black people come to Afrika to reside; instead of taking the European approach of destroying trees and nature to build, that we may instead build state-of-the-art tree homes. By doing this we may implement embracing the beauty of the planet while being technologically inclined as a species. There is no reason why people cannot harness the fruits of technology and nature at the very same time. And whether or not I get the chance to implement this idea or someone else does; it does not matter to me, because I know that either way it will be done for the sake of Afrika and its people, which is the ultimate goal.

The future of Afrika is very bright, as you will see; it is up to you if you will be a contributor of that bright future. I hope you have enjoyed the depths of this eBook based on the heart, effort, and commitment I put into it for my brothers and sisters of the world to use as a basic blueprint to our forward progression. I leave you with this video to get a better insight of the open arms and innovation waiting for you in **Afrika: Blacks Without Borders: Full Movie** Length 01:10:51

###

Note to Readers

Malcolm X and Mandela: By any means necessary Length 01:20

Our time is now my brothers and sisters. Let us unite under one cause, under one heart and under one global nation. I am glad to see that so many black people are waking up; so many black people are gaining knowledge and communicating through social networks; and so many black people now understand who they are. Let's continue on and learn from the leaders who have gone before us:

"Rather than there being **one** who is **uniting we**; **we** are instead **uniting** as **one**." ~ Odaine Tomlinson

Connect With Odaine Tomlinson

Instagram @ A.Real.Man or on Facebook